HOW IT HAPPENS
at the Boat Factory

By Dawn Frederick

Photographs by Bob and Diane Wolfe

CLARA HOUSE BOOKS

Minneapolis

The publisher would like to thank Crestliner, Inc., and its employees for their generous help with this book.

Copyright ©2002 by Clara House Books, a division of The Oliver Press, Inc.

Clara House Books
The Oliver Press, Inc.
Charlotte Square
5707 West 36th Street
Minneapolis, MN 55416-2510

Library of Congress Cataloging-in-Publication Data
Frederick, Dawn, 1975-
   How it happens at the boat factory / by Dawn Frederick ; photographs by Bob and Diane Wolfe.
     p. cm. — (How it happens)
  Summary: Photographs and text describe how aluminum boats are made.
  ISBN 1-881508-90-0 (lib. bdg.)
  1. Boatbuilding—Juvenile literature. 2. Boatyards—Juvenile literature. [1. Boatbuilding.
2. Boatyards.] I. Wolfe, Robert L., ill. II. Wolfe, Diane, ill. III. Title. IV. Series.

VM321 .F668 2002
623.8'3—dc21

2001053927

ISBN 1-881508-90-0
Printed in the United States of America
08 07 06 05 04 03 02   8 7 6 5 4 3 2 1

Imagine cruising across a big blue lake on a warm summer day. Maybe you're about to go fishing or waterskiing, or perhaps you're just enjoying the feeling of the wind on your face as your boat speeds through the water. How can a factory transform thin sheets of metal into a boat that can carry you on a lake, river, or ocean? In this book, you'll see step by step how one company builds boats that bring people hours of summer fun.

Aluminum

This factory makes boats out of **aluminum**—the same soft, lightweight metal used in soda cans. Each huge roll of aluminum, like the one shown at right, weighs between 2,500 and 3,500 pounds. The factory uses a total of 6 million pounds of aluminum every year!

The machine shown above, called an **uncoiler-leveler**, gradually unrolls the thin, flexible sheet of aluminum and flattens it so it can be cut.

Next, the aluminum goes into the **flying shear**, which works like a giant scissors. Its two sharp blades snip the metal into smaller, rectangular sheets.

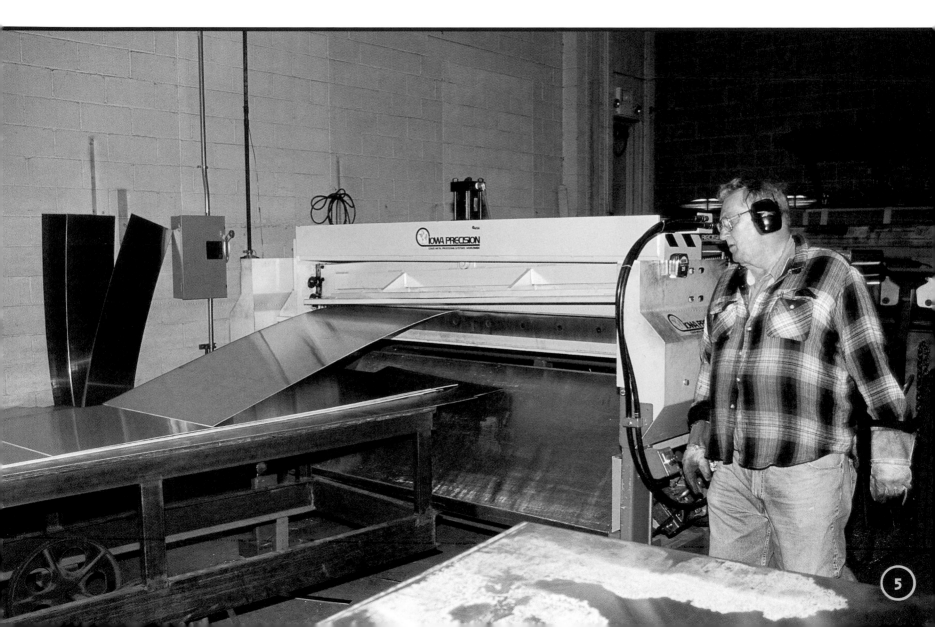

The Router

A machine called a **router** cuts the aluminum into the different shapes needed to build a boat. Several sheets of aluminum are stacked on top of each other and nailed together to keep them from slipping around. Then the router cuts through all of them at once.

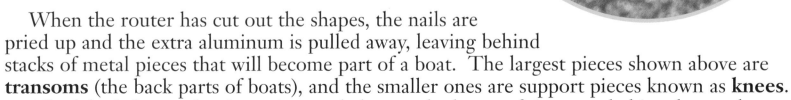

When the router has cut out the shapes, the nails are pried up and the extra aluminum is pulled away, leaving behind stacks of metal pieces that will become part of a boat. The largest pieces shown above are **transoms** (the back parts of boats), and the smaller ones are support pieces known as **knees**.

All of the leftover aluminum is recycled, even the heaps of tiny metal chips shown above right. The factory recycles about one million pounds of aluminum each year.

Press Brakes

Since not all parts of a boat are flat, some of the flat aluminum pieces have to be bent to make them the right shape. A machine called a **press brake** clamps down tightly on part of a piece of aluminum, bending it into the shape needed to build the boat.

The piece being bent above is a **bulkhead**, which will support the floor of the boat. The press brake at top right bends metal pieces into a curve to create **bottom stiffeners**, the parts that will support the bottom of the boat. The one at bottom right makes creases in the large pieces of aluminum that will become the **hull**—the main body of the boat.

Welding

Now the different pieces of the boat are welded together. **Welding** is a way of joining pieces of metal by heating them at the spot where they meet. When the metal cools and hardens, the pieces will be firmly attached to each other, as shown at left. Above, bottom stiffeners are being welded to the hull bottom.

Once the bottom stiffeners have been attached, the hull pieces are placed on a boat-shaped frame called a **hull jig**. The jig will hold the parts of the hull together until they are welded.

The four pieces that make up the hull are welded together with a **pacer**, a welding tool that can make long, continuous welds down the whole length of the boat. The pacer moves along the ceiling on a track, following the worker as he moves.

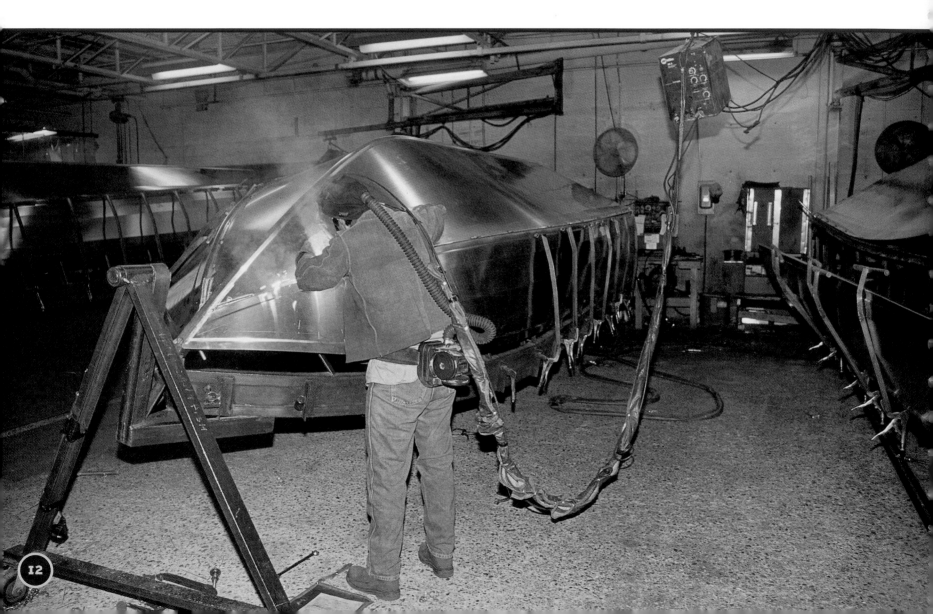

Once the basic body of the boat is complete, it is removed from the hull jig and turned right side up. Other aluminum pieces, like the bulkheads that will support the floor, are welded onto the inside of the boat, as shown above.

Some parts of the boat are welded together by a **robot**, a machine that can be programmed to perform complicated physical tasks. In the picture at right, the robot is working on a piece that will be welded inside the **bow**, or front, of the boat.

Sanding

After all the pieces of the boat have been welded together, workers use pneumatic (air-powered) sanders to smooth the surface of the aluminum in the same way that sandpaper smoothes rough wood. Sanding the boat makes it look its best after it is painted. A smooth metal surface also helps the finished boat move more easily through the water.

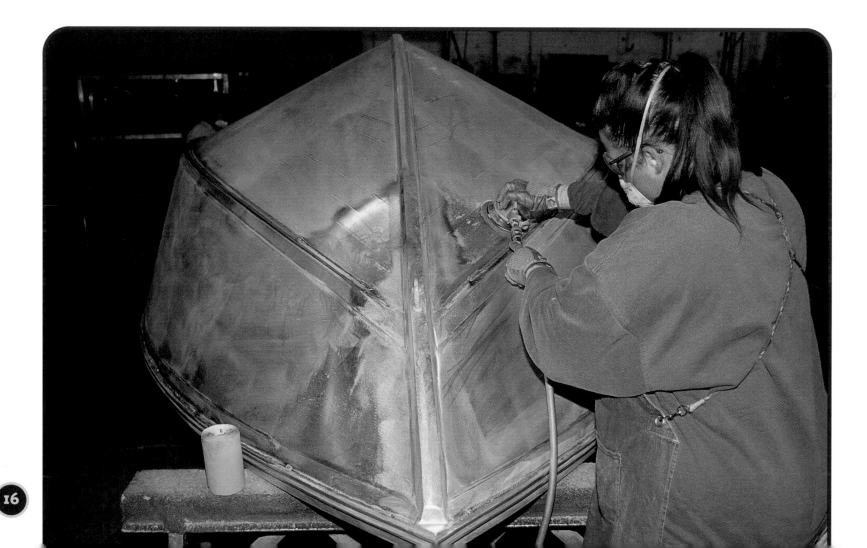

Testing for Leaks

Each weld on the boat is carefully inspected to make sure it is watertight. The boat is tested for leaks by being lowered into a pool of water, right in the middle of the factory. If any water leaks into the boat, a worker uses an air wand—a machine that makes a fast, strong stream of air—to blow the water out of the way so he can see which seam is leaking. Any leaky seams are re-welded. Otherwise, so much water could leak into the boat that it might sink in the middle of a river or lake!

Paint

The picture at left shows a worker (wearing a protective suit) using a spray gun to cover a boat with a coat of white paint. The painted boats are placed in a large oven, as shown below, and heated to 425 degrees Fahrenheit for about 20 minutes. The heat of the oven "cures" the paint, drying it into a hard surface that won't peel or scratch off easily.

Next, the boat is decorated with a stripe of brightly colored paint. A worker outlines the shape of the stripe with masking tape. Since the rest of the boat will remain white, it is covered up with paper to protect it from the colored paint. After the colored paint is sprayed onto the exposed part of the boat, the boat goes back into the oven to cure.

Decals

The company labels and decorates its boats with **decals**, designs that are transferred from special paper. The paper is smoothed onto the side of the boat and wetted down with water. When the paper is peeled away, the design remains stuck to the surface of the boat.

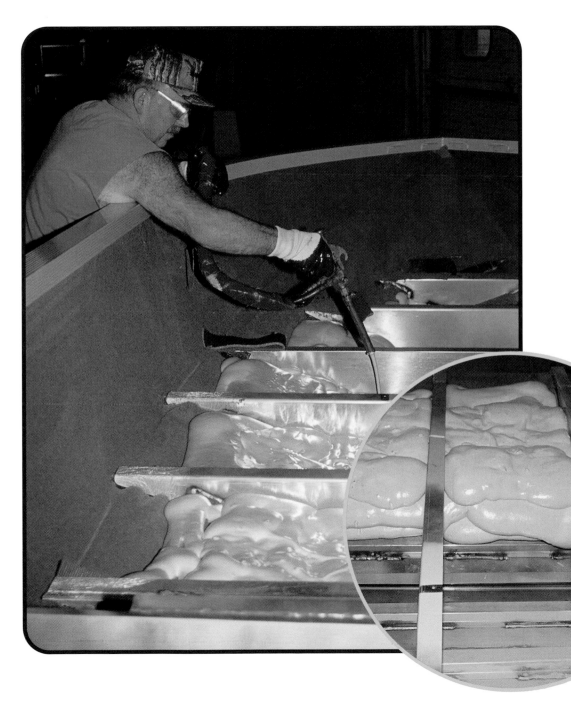

Flotation Foam

The bottom of the boat is filled with **flotation foam** to make it **buoyant** (able to float in water). The foam is heated to about 130 degrees Fahrenheit, turning it into a creamy liquid that is poured inside the boat. As it cures, it will expand and harden into a solid foam that is lighter than water, helping the boat to stay on top of the water instead of sinking to the bottom.

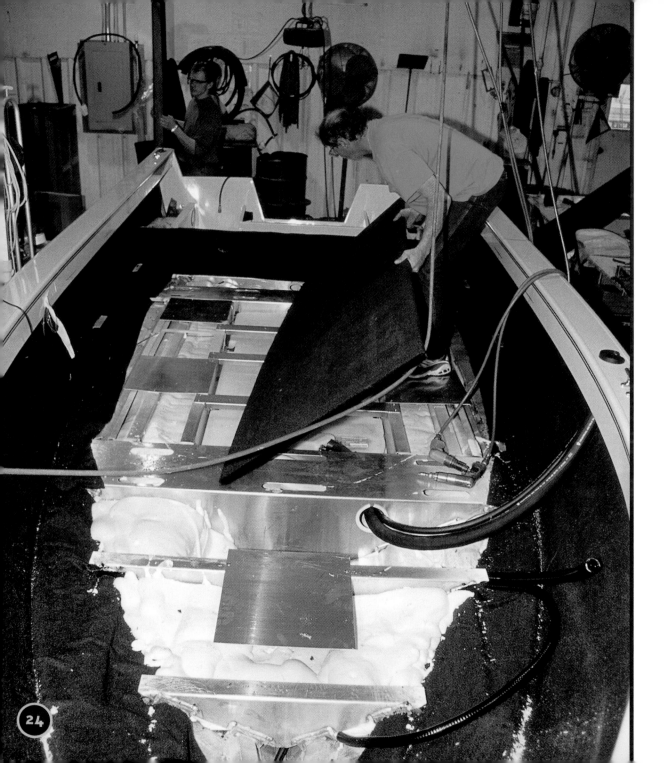

The Floor

After the flotation foam has cooled and hardened, panels are placed over it to make the floor of the boat. The panels have been covered in carpet to make the floor more colorful and more comfortable for the boat's passengers.

Upholstery

Meanwhile, in the factory's **upholstery** department, fabric is measured, cut, and sewn to decorate the inside of the boat and make it more comfortable.

The worker shown on the bottom right is cutting **vinyl** (a tough, flexible plastic) into pieces that will be used to cover the seats of the boat. Wearing a chain-metal glove to protect her left hand, she uses a machine with a sharp blade that moves up and down very fast to saw through about 30 pieces of vinyl at once.

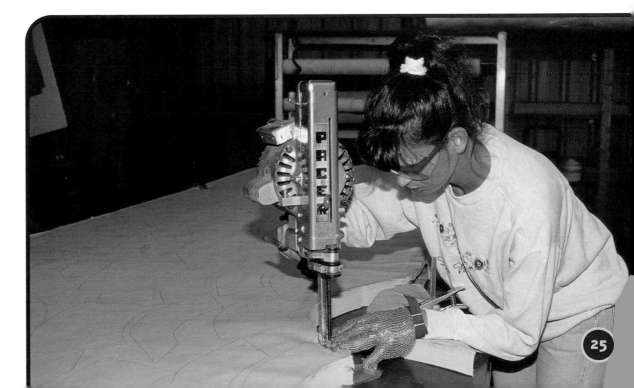

Workers use sewing machines to sew the pieces of vinyl together into seat covers.

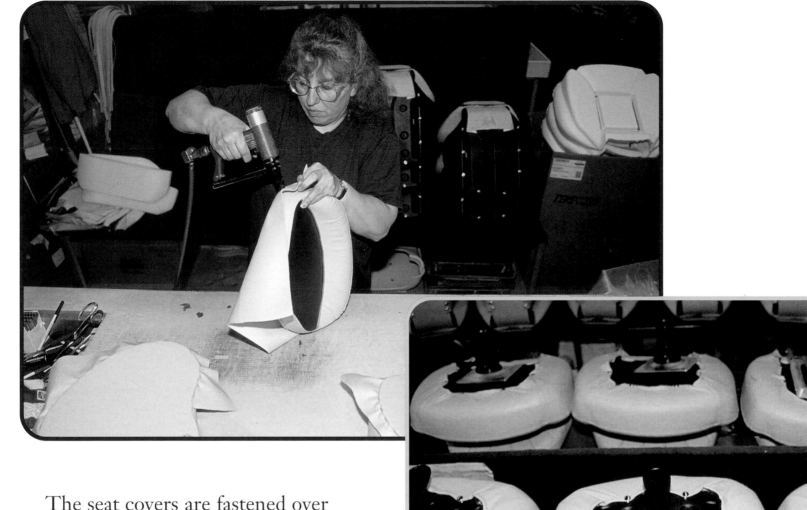

The seat covers are fastened over foam cushions on plastic frames, and the seats are ready to go into the boat.

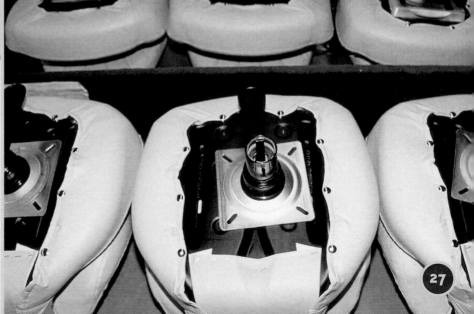

Finishing

Many of the accessories that allow us to drive boats from place to place and to ride in them comfortably aren't added to the boat until it is almost complete. During this part of the boat-making process (called finishing), the motor is installed, as shown at left. The picture below shows the steering wheel and instrument panels after they have been added to the boat. The seats will be installed into the round metal bases visible on the floor.

y

The factory makes different **models**, or styles, of boats. They are different colors and sizes, and may have special features like windshields, stereos, and fishing-rod holders. Since the boats can be so different, workers check every boat to make sure all the correct parts have been included. Then they carefully vacuum and clean the boat to get it ready for its new owner.

Finally, the boats are loaded onto a truck that will take them to one of many boat dealerships (stores) around the country. There, they will be sold to customers eager to fish, swim, waterski—or just cruise around a beautiful lake in a brand-new boat.

Glossary

aluminum: a soft, lightweight metal

bottom stiffener: a long, curved strip of metal that supports the bottom of a boat

bow: the front of a boat

bulkhead: a piece of metal that supports the floor of a boat

buoyant: able to float in water

decal: a design that is transferred from special paper onto materials such as glass or metal

flotation foam: a lightweight foam that is placed in the bottom of a boat to help make it more buoyant

flying shear: a machine that cuts a sheet of aluminum into smaller pieces

hull: the main body of a boat

hull jig: the frame that holds pieces of the hull together while they are being welded

knees: small support pieces in a boat

model: a style or design of an item

pacer: a kind of welding tool that can make long, continuous welds

press brake: a machine that helps to bend pieces of aluminum by clamping down on them

robot: a machine that can be programmed to perform complicated physical tasks

router: a machine that cuts out pieces of different shapes from a sheet of aluminum

transom: a piece that forms part of the back of a boat

uncoiler-leveler: a machine that unrolls a roll of aluminum and holds it flat so it can be cut

upholstery: the fabric and other materials used in cushions and furniture

vinyl: a tough, flexible plastic

welding: a way of joining pieces of metal by heating them at the spot where they meet